First published in Great Britain in 1995 by Andersen Press Ltd., 20 Vauxhall Bridge Road, London SW1V 2SA.  Published in Australia by Random House
Australia Pty., 20 Alfred Street, Milsons Point, Sydney, NSW 2061.  All rights reserved.  Colour separated in Switzerland by Photolitho AG,
Offsetreproduktionen, Gossau, Zürich.  Printed and bound in Italy by Grafiche AZ, Verona.

10   9   8   7   6   5   4   3   2   1

British Library Cataloguing in Publication Data available.

ISBN  0 86264 627 8

*This book has been printed on acid-free paper*

# A FLEA IN THE EAR

By Stephen Wyllie
Illustrated by Ken Brown

Andersen Press • London

ONE MOONLIT NIGHT, as the spotted dog was lifting the flaps on the side of the chicken coop to make sure the hens were all tucked up in bed, he heard a twig snap in the woods nearby.

"I know you're out there, fox," he barked. "Stay away from my hens."

"Good evening," said the wily fox politely, sauntering
leisurely into the farmyard.
"Back off," said the dog, "or I'll bite."
"You can't imagine for one moment that I would dream of taking
one of your scrawny hens," lied the fox. "I much prefer a nice, fat
juicy duck."

"Well, that's all right then," said the dog, scratching his fleas.
"Just remember what I said."
"I will," said the fox, edging closer. "I see you have a spot of flea trouble."
"Don't talk about it," said the dog. "At this time of year it's agony."

"I never have any trouble myself," said the fox. "But then I know the secret that keeps them at bay."

"What? You do?" asked the dog eagerly. "Please tell me."

"I couldn't possibly," the fox replied. "It's a family secret, handed down from father to son for generations."

"Oh, please tell," pleaded the dog. "I'll give anything to get rid of my fleas."
"Anything?" asked the fox slyly.
"Well, almost anything."
"I suppose I might be persuaded in exchange for five or six of your stringy birds."

"Definitely not," said the dog indignantly. "I'd lose my job."
"Oh well," said the fox, "suit yourself. Bye bye."
And he left the unhappy dog to scratch away for the rest of the night.

The following afternoon the fox came back.

"Good afternoon," he said.

"Hello," growled the dog, suspiciously.

"I've been thinking things over," said the fox, "and have decided to tell you the secret for nothing. I couldn't allow a fellow creature to suffer so much pain."

"That's wonderful," said the dog. "What do I have to do?"

"It's quite simple really. You just trot over the hill, down the other side, through the gate and along the lane until you come to a pond. Walk into the water and, as it gets deeper, the fleas will climb up your legs. Eventually, only your head will be dry and all the fleas will be on it. Take a deep breath and dunk your head under the water and all your fleas will drown."

"Brilliant," said the dog. "I'm surprised I never thought of it myself."
"Off you go then," said the fox. "I'll watch the chickens while
you're away. Just think of it, flea free for the first time in your life."
"I can hardly wait," said the dog, and he galloped off up the hill,
down to the gate, and along to the pond to drown his fleas.

As he lowered himself into the water, he was astonished to hear a voice in his ear.

"I know you are about to drown us," said a flea, "but if you go back to the bank, we will all jump off and promise never to bite you again."

The dog paused for a moment.

"Oh, very well. So long as you keep your word."

He walked back to the bank and all the fleas leapt off. The happy dog went home. When he got back, he found that the fox had vanished and when he lifted the flaps he discovered that his hens had too.

"Oh no," howled the dog. "I'll lose my job, I'll be homeless."
He lay down in despair. When he felt a little better, he noticed a
trail of feathers leading into the wood.

He got up and followed it until he came at last to the fox's den.
He knocked on the door. The fox opened it.
"Hello," he said, feigning surprise. "What brings you here?"
"I just dropped by," said the dog, pretending to scratch, "to tell you
that I went for your flea cure, but I couldn't get into the pond.

It was full to the brim with fat, juicy ducks."

"It was?" asked the fox, licking his lips.

"Overflowing," lied the dog. "I'll try again later when they have gone. Bye bye."

"Goodbye," said the fox, and closed the door.

The dog hid behind a tree. He hadn't waited long before the fox came out of his den with an empty sack slung over his shoulder. After a quick look round, he slunk off towards the pond...

...only to find when he got there, that there wasn't a trace of the fat, juicy ducks the dog had said he'd seen. While he sat there in disbelief, all the fleas who had so nearly drowned leapt joyfully, but unnoticed, on to his back.

Meanwhile, the dog had broken down the fox's door and there, sure enough, he found a squawking bagful of his chickens. He gathered them up and took them back to their coop, determined never to let them out of his sight again.